a b u

M e l a n i e   C l a r k e

The contents of this book is based on my real life story. It's from all the experiences I have faced. I couldn't tell anyone, so I told my diary but now this diary has become my book. I have written this book to encourage others to seek help. If you are in a similar situation, please seek help, I did!! This was my life!

Foreword

Looking back, I cannot believe I lived a day of it. Have you ever felt like you're stuck in a rut and can't begin to find your way out, no family to speak to because you're either embarrassed or ashamed or feel like people will not understand?

I don't want to tell people because I know I'm not strong enough to leave. If I go back to him, people will worry about me, especially my family. I used to feel so guilty when they would worry because I knew, due to my decisions, they would have sleepless nights. That made me feel so bad inside.

I thought people would be angry or disappointed in me. Let's face it: I'm sick of repeating the same thing in my mind, much less for other people to listen to it all.

I want to walk away from this life. I feel so unhappy. Every day, I wake up feeling like I'm dying inside, tired of smiling through it all for the sake of the children, living most days with anger, hurt, resentment, anxiety and, most importantly, guilt.

Abused

Let's reflect on this for a moment. How can someone that loves you want to make you feel worthless, like you're worth absolutely nothing? Sometimes, our own feelings we have at that particular time become confused with the reality of the situation. We lose sight of what's normal as they have you so sucked in. You find yourself unable to either think or function the way in which you normally would when it comes to handling situations.

Guilt

The guilt of knowing you are tolerating this life, knowing you are letting your children be subjected to it emotionally, but in the same breath living in constant denial, hanging on to this happy family vision: I can help him be a better person vision; he will one day change and it will get better vision.

Anxiety

Not knowing what mood he is going to be in. Will he be nice to me today? Will he pick a fight today, and will he put me down, criticise me, and make trivial things into a big episode? These things would stress me out; he was a difficult person to be around.

Resentment

Knowing the type of strong, confident person I once was, who was always smiling, has somehow been chipped away day by day by this one person. The person I am is someone who comes from a loving, happy family that has always shown love. I couldn't actually have asked for a better childhood.

We were always happy, and still are. I was brought up to love myself, respect myself. *What* happened to Mel? *Who* is Mel? Can I get her back? There was a huge amount of resentment when I looked at him because of the things he had done. I began disliking him as a person the majority of the time.

Hurt

How can he say he loves me and treat me like this? Is he really sorry? I can't forgive him for the things he has done yet still I keep him there because it hurts too much to accept that this is what he is and will forever be.

It hurts too much to let this 'me and him' thing go completely.

"He's never going to leave me alone anyway, so what's the point?"

"He's going to call me repeatedly, ring my doorbell, cry and get people he knew to speak to me."

"He's going to wear me down emotionally until I cave in like I normally do."

Make me feel sorry for him, play on his awful childhood memories about being abused by his parents, use the children to manipulate me into feeling bad, purposely make his presentation scruffy so I'd think he was depressed and couldn't cope without me.

When I would leave my home to do the school run I would find him asleep in his car day and night until I spoke to him. Later on, I got to find out he wanted me to feel guilty for leaving him.

Anger

He looked at me like I was nothing when he became violent. He would make me feel defenceless.

"I hate you!"

"You bitch!"

"All you do is cause problems!"

"You're dumb!"

"You will never be as intelligent as I am!"

"You need to learn to respect your man."

"Even my kids know what you're like."

"You can't do anything."

"Any man that has you will only want to f*** you!"

"You don't have nothing else going for you."

"My GCSE results were better than yours."

"Why don't you disappear?"

"Shut your mouth!"

"If you speak again, see what I do to you, little girl."

"Don't move!"

"Say sorry!"

"What's wrong with you?"

He would ask me questions for hours while leaving me locked in a room and, no matter what the answer was, he would hurt me by pushing me into the wall and furniture repeatedly, push his knuckles into my jaw or my cheeks, squeezing them into my face. During this time, he would come up close and whisper, "I could break every bone in your face if I punched you. You couldn't get back up, nor could you do anything about it. I could do that if I wanted."

He would slap my head over and over again and drag me around by my ankles on the carpet. I still have carpet burns on my elbows. He would choke me and hold me on the ground by my hair while shouting questions at me.

"Why do you cause so many problems?"

"Why don't you go and kill yourself?"

"Do you know how angry you have made me?"

Afterwards, all my joints would feel so sore; my face, my neck, my arms especially would ache for days at a time.

Further intimidating behaviour towards me would consist of him shouting loudly in my face with his nose touching mine and his hands spread apart, verbally threatening me by saying things like:

"I am going to kill you if I hear you speak to me like that again."

"If I was to deal with you, you would be dead."

"You leave me and I will kill you."

During the attacks, he would play mind games with me. He would consider "Yes I agree" to mean I'm taking him for a fool. "I don't agree with you" would be a violation, considering I caused all the problems. Not saying anything and believing that this was a safer option would mean:

"You think you are big and bad; you think you can ignore me again.

"I'm going to show you the meaning of pain. You've never been beaten, trying to walk around crying wolf, making it out like you're some kind of battered woman."

"If I put my hands on you, you would be dead."

"You're going to leave me now, aren't you? Say it! Go on! Well, I have nothing to lose, so let's go! If you make me repeat myself, I'm going to choke the living day lights out of you!"

Humiliation

He would speak badly of me to his family and friends, and lie about what he had said or done to me before them. I used to find it strange because he loved playing happy families in front of them, then on other occasions he would pick on me in front of his family.

He even tried to physically fight me in front of them and then tell them how much he loved me afterwards. Most of the things he was doing weren't a secret. All his family was very manipulative; they knew what he was doing to me, but, so long as it wasn't them dealing with it, they were pretty much happy.

His family played a huge part in it. They would come to my home and speak on his behalf. When they came round, I would tell them everything he was doing to me. They also saw the bruises and scratches on my body. They would ask him if what I was saying was true, and he would make up a whole load of excuses for his behaviour. Sometimes, he would tell the truth; mostly, he would play it down. They would listen to his long discussions, encourage me to stay with him and work things out, and then they would leave him in my house and go.

After he had abused me one day, he decided to call his mother to ask her to come round to my home. Whenever she arrived, she would give me this look. The look she gave said that I had done something wrong. It was an irritated, pissed-off sort of look. I said to her, "You seem upset with me like I have done something wrong." She had a surprised expression on her face and an odd laugh because she wasn't used to me speaking up to her. Her reply was, "You haven't done anything." These were the sort of mind games she would play.

I was always polite to his family, and I never spoke up for myself even when I could see what they were doing. I feel this is because I was emotionally exhausted dealing with him; I couldn't take on his family as well. I felt like not only was he in my head but his family was too. They were very controlling; like him. They had a way of making me feel like they cared about me and my kids. They did whatever it took to make me feel that at certain times that they were genuinely supportive and had my and the kids' interest at heart, but what I couldn't see at that time was how much they were manipulating me.

I would make the decision to leave him and try and not let him suck me back in, then his mother would do things like invite me over for dinner. I would find him there when I arrived. She would have purposely planned it so that she could get me and him to sort things out.

"He loves you."

"He needs help."

"Maybe you and him should go to counselling together."

They would make lots of efforts to call me repeatedly to see how things were going.

"Is he trying?"

They manipulated me into thinking and feeling that this life their son was offering me was a normal life. I was lower than I had ever been, and it was obvious to them. They saw what his bullying was doing to me, and how out of control the physical abuse was but, no matter what, they still encouraged me to remain in the situation. I stopped smiling, laughing, dressing up; I even stopped speaking whenever I was around him and his family. What was the point of being happy? Give it five minutes, the smile would be taken off my face. When I was with my own family and friends, I felt like there was still some of the old Mel there. I felt so at peace; I guess that was where I could get some peace.

"I used to love him"

We met when I was 14. My first love. I was still in school; I hadn't even taken my GCSEs yet. He was my only love. Back then, he was very family orientated. Guys that liked me back then didn't look as if they want something serious. I guess that's what drew me to him.

He brought me to his home and introduced me to his family. I already knew them because they knew my family. Everyone was connected from when I was small so he was told to treat me well because it would reflect badly on the family.

I come from a decent family and my family is a close unit. I was not streetwise or experienced. Mostly, I would be home with my family unless I was meeting up with close friends. During this time, I was studying Graphic Design at Carshalton College and working part time at Pilot Clothing. I was very young and was still not one hundred per cent sure of what I wanted to do; I was still on my course, doing different work placements.

The day I met him, I brought him home. My mum and my two brothers were there. I had a friend who happened to often call me; this friend was a guy and had been my friend for a long time. I had done nothing wrong. He called round and, in my family's home, raised his voice, telling me he did not like the idea of another guy calling me, then accusing me of being up to something.

My mum told him she did not appreciate him raising his voice in her home and that she found him disrespectful. From that day, my family did not like him, plain and simple. They could see through him and the 'gentleman's act' he liked to portray. If this didn't ring alarm bells for me to see that this guy was no good, I don't know what would!

Back then, I was so into him that I ignored this. I should have known from what happened on that day that he was no good for me. He had no respect, behaving like that for my family to hear. It also showed a lot about his family life. When you are young and dating someone, sometimes you don't think about the long term; just the now! I never really thought about what having children or a future with someone like this could bring my way.

He would call me and invite me to every family function. We spent nearly every day together. I got into a serious relationship way to young, especially as he was very jealous and controlling. He would call me repeatedly and interrogate me. My family tried to tell me but I was too young to see the bigger picture.

Him calling me constantly, interrogating my whereabouts was his way of making me feel loved. While he was doing this, he was cheating and lying at every opportunity he got; I just didn't know it at the time. The more my family was against it, the less I listened to them. I'd been brought up with old-fashioned values and I wanted a relationship with someone I could see having a future with although I was very young.

My First Born

I was eighteen years old and was still seeing him. I was so into him and would bend over backwards to do nice things for him, like when he was sick I would cook something nice and get a cab to wherever he was to bring it to him. He used to work in Kentish Town and I would leave whatever it was I was doing countless times and get a train from south London to meet him for lunch to bring him lunch money when he didn't have any. I really loved and cared for him very much; would have given the world for him.

I was still at the stage where I was making friends through work, as well as with friends of friends. I got to the stage where I distanced myself from my male friends because he made an issue whenever they called. I soon stopped speaking to them all altogether as I couldn't take the arguments. In his mind, every guy that was my friend wanted to be romantically involved with me. I never let go of my female friends, of which I had a lot.

I was still living at home with my family and, even though I wanted to be with him, I felt like I was missing out on having my freedom. Sometimes, as much as I wanted to be with him, I wanted to breathe again; being so young. He constantly said he wanted to have a child with me. "Imagine how that would be?" But I didn't want children, being so young, although I said someday I would like to have a family with him.

I was on the mini pill because the combined pill was causing health problems for me. One morning, I woke up for work and felt very weak. Near to the end of my shift, I asked my manager if I could leave early because I felt sick. I walked outside and I remember thinking that my period was a day or two late and it started playing on my mind that I could be pregnant. I decided to go to the walk-in clinic where they did free tests. I didn't call him or anyone else because I felt a bit silly and figured that I was being paranoid.

When I was told that I was six weeks pregnant, the panic kicked in. My mum and dad were in the West Indies at this time and had left me with my big brother. I was terrified as to what they would say and how they would react; I felt like I had let them down. I was supposed to know better, having seen the bad choices my mum, brothers and my older sisters had made in their own lives.

I called him and told him, and he said, "This is great news!" He wanted to celebrate.

When my parents came back from Jamaica, I had to tell them. In the end, I had my sister tell them because I was too scared to do it myself. The way my dad looked at me made me feel ashamed of my pregnancy. I felt that I had truly let them down.

Despite the fact that being pregnant so young wasn't the greatest thing, I loved my baby very much and was going to keep it, no matter what anyone said. He was happy, and he made it known to me and his family. Things were nice for a few weeks, but that all changed.

From the day that I told him I was pregnant my 'journey' began. He promised to look after me and take me from my family's home as soon as he got the money together. "Before the baby is born I will get a place for us," he said. He promised to save and provide for the baby.

He spent most of his time drifting from job to job, making empty promises, disrespecting me before his friends and family. He started to behave very coldly towards me when we argued. I slowly began to see the real him.

Today's my very first scan for the baby. We are not speaking again. "Congratulations, Miss Clarke. It's a boy." When we left the scan room, he stood there with a smirk on his face. "Come here, give me a cuddle."

"No!"

"That's okay because it's a boy and he won't want to live with you. When he's born I will take him away from you!"

He walked away and left me on the street. From the day I had told him I was pregnant he changed towards me.

He was horrible to me in different kinds of ways: his attitude and behaviour were different; if we disagreed about anything, he wouldn't speak about it with me; he would mock me, laugh and walk off; he would talk down to me and stop making any effort to be nice; he became very cruel and looked for any excuse to argue. As a result, we argued a lot.

When my son was born, I lost a lot of weight because I had lost my appetite. I had no support from him when I needed it; never feeling I could rely on him. I also couldn't rely on him to look after the baby because he was so irresponsible. He was always tired and did nothing to help with the baby unless he felt like it. During our arguments, he would snatch the baby from me, shout in my face, then disappear for days at a time and not call. The list was endless. Around this time, I became very stressed and tired; I went from a size twelve to a size eight. He gave me no financial or emotional support. Lucky for me, I had my family to help me when I was unwell, and they would look after my son and buy him clothes and food, etc.

The Blessing

I organised my son's blessing alone because he was trying to bully me into blessing him at a Seventh Day Adventist church. When I disagreed, he chose to behave distantly and unsupportive. He wasn't the sort of person who would sit down and have a discussion and reach a compromise to suit the both of us; it was always his way. He didn't help fund the occasion but he wanted to bully me into doing everything his way when my parents were paying for everything and he hadn't paid one penny towards his son's blessing. As a result, my parents helped me prepare, decorate and fund the celebration.

I held my son at the front of the church next to the godparents I chose for him, slowly watching all my family and friends arriving. My mum was so hurt to see that he hadn't shown up and had left me standing alone, so she had my dad stand beside me. One hour later, he came strolling through the church door.

The thing about christenings, birthdays and Christmas is that they are special occasions; moments you can't get back!

That day was very humiliating because all my family talked about him arriving late as well as his family's lack of enthusiasm to take pictures and socialise; they were all very rude. I felt embarrassed and shown up in front of my family.

I kept on pushing and pushing myself to ignore the bad stuff, and kidding myself that I would one day be happy and that the bad times wouldn't last forever. One day he would realise what he had.

He became confrontational during arguments, pushing me around, and then he would cry afterwards, promising not to let it happen again.

Pregnancy Number Two

I was happy for one week exactly. Then he changed. He became really aggressive, pushing, grabbing, threatening, shoving and slamming me into walls. Once, he slammed me against the washing machine repeatedly while choking me.

I remember he used to come round to my home and constantly leave my place extremely untidy. One day, I told him to stop doing it; I had enough to do that he wasn't helping me with. He became violent and bent my arm up behind my back.

On another occasion, he behaved so badly, shouting at me because I interrupted him while he was speaking, that he attacked me in my house. I had to lie to him after enduring being locked in a room for hours just so that he would leave. My son was in the room while his dad was shouting. My son didn't say anything; he just sat there watching TV and glancing every so often at his dad.

I called his sister, and when she arrived he became extremely irrational. I told him he was lucky I had called his family and not mine. He ran across the room and threw me against the wall, holding me by my throat with one hand. His sister was very shocked. Then he started begging me in front of her, saying he was sorry. "I love you. Please don't look at me like that. I didn't mean it."

She called his brother because she was shocked and didn't know what to do. Once his brother arrived, he came back in, then went straight back outside for a cigarette. That night, his brother and sister left him in my home.

He would always be sorry, grab on to my legs, begging me to give him one more chance. "I promise I will get help. I can't live without you. If you say it's over, I'm going in that kitchen right now and I'm going to get something to end my own life."

This sort of thing was a big part of his game of manipulation. Sometimes, when things were good between us, I would feel like I was happy, and this is how I wanted things to always be, but I didn't realise back then that, deep down, the relationship had ended for me already; I just couldn't see it.

I woke up Christmas morning, heavily pregnant and alone with my son. I sat and opened my son's gifts with him because his dad hadn't shown up. No phone call, nothing.

He then appeared on Christmas evening. I didn't say two words to him and he didn't say two words to me.

This continued up to New Year's Eve. As the time approached twelve o'clock, I could hear fireworks going off and people cheering outside. I sat on one side of the settee and he sat on the other in silence watching the TV. I was so hurt I got up quietly and went to bed alone.

With regard to his disappearing act, he offered no explanation or showed me any respect. A few weeks later, I found out he had cheated on me and that's why he didn't spend Christmas with me and our son. After finding out that he had cheated, I couldn't bring myself to speak to him. He was prepared to risk everything for someone who, in his words, meant nothing.

I couldn't understand how he could put me through this. Every night, I would sit on the floor in the corner of my bedroom and cry. Through my tears, it helped to realise the pain I was feeling.

During the day, I was a happy, fun mummy for my son. I would take him swimming; interacted as much as possible with him. I didn't want him to know something was wrong or feel the badness of the situation. What was playing on my mind the most was the guilt of knowing that I had no strength to change my life, which made me feel like the worst mum in the world.

Knowing he had cheated was hard to take. I refused to speak to him. When I came home one time, he had let himself in through my back door with his 'secret' key and begged me to forgive him. This went on up to a few weeks before I gave birth. Being pregnant again made it hard to leave. He grovelled and grovelled until I gave in.

He would show up here and there to try and talk but I was too tired to bother. After my daughter was born, he ran around my house tidying up while his family was present.

Many times during this period I tried to get on with it and live my life but he never left me alone. I thought to myself, I'm already pregnant again, so what's the point? I've already gone and made life ten times harder for myself, so why bother? Might as well stick it out.

His family would come round unannounced after I gave birth. He behaved like he wanted to make up for what he had done and would help out round my house and be over nice to me. This went on for a few weeks after the birth, and then slowly everything went back to normal.

First Home Memories

The violence was too much to bear and, because I knew deep down I wasn't strong enough, I decided I had to keep going for my children's sake, so I decided to move house. I went on to the Home Swapper site. After a few weeks, I found a match. At the time, I was living in a two-bedroom house with a garden. This was my first home and I truly loved it. It had a large living room and dining room, a large bathroom, and the bedrooms were a reasonable size.

It was a hard decision but at this point I cared more about getting myself and the kids away from him and the situation than keeping my beautiful house. Leaving behind the bad memories of that house would be good for me anyway.

I spoke to a lady a few weeks later and went with my mum to view her home in South Croydon. She had a ground floor maisonette with two bedrooms and a gorgeous garden. It was a very neat place with reasonably sized rooms. What I really liked was where it was situated; it was at the top of a hill and the view was beautiful; quiet and peaceful. Yep, this is what me and the kids needed. Later on, the kids and I could get somewhere bigger again. Once

I had accepted the property, I changed the kid's schools and prepared for the move.

I kept the move quiet; the only people who knew were my family. I didn't want him finding out while I was waiting to move, and at this point I told him it was over.

I changed my telephone number and tried to get on with my life but he would sit in his car outside the kids' school until I walked past and he would follow me home. He would then knock on my door repeatedly for hours.

One day, I went into the kitchen to make some food. I had arranged to meet my mum and stay with her, as I felt very edgy. I knew he was watching the house although I hadn't seen him, and I also knew that he was going to find a way of getting in. When I looked up, he was standing at my kitchen window looking really rough. He told me that he had slept in my garden all night, waiting for me to come back so that he could speak to me.

I had already opened my kitchen window before I was aware he was there. When I looked up and saw him standing there it scared the living day lights out of me! He stood there, crying and begging me to let him in so that we could talk. "I want to see my son" was just an excuse to get inside. I told him now was not a good time and that he should go, but he never took no for an answer; he just went on and on. I tried to close the window. He prised it open with his fingers every time, crying, begging me and becoming really intense.

Then he jumped through my kitchen window and started chasing me. I ran towards the front door to get help, but he grabbed me with both hands and threw me down into the passageway, slamming the front door shut. I remember closing my eyes, leaning against the wall, feeling as though I was breaking down inside with fear. I managed to calm him down so that I could get out of the house.

As soon as I met my mum, I broke down. "I'm not going back home. I'm staying with you!" I stayed with her for two to three weeks, which would bring me up to my moving date. I was too afraid to go home on my own, so one night before my moving date my mum came with me to check on my home and pick up some more clothes. I went upstairs and packed while she checked the doors and windows.

All the windows in the property were double-glazed. As my mum pulled on the handle of the small window in my kitchen, it started to come away. She called me and we both realised that he had used a tool to loosen the window to let himself in and out. Later, when I asked him why he had done it he said, "Do you know how long it's been like that? I came in at night when you were sleeping!"

He never thought that what he did was strange. He never found his behaviour a sign for needing help. He never even stopped to think about the danger he had put me or the children in.

When I told him that I needed to change my life, move, change my number, he would sit outside in his car and further harass me, knocking on my door and following me, saying, "I'm sorry! I had no idea what I was doing to you. It's going to be different!"

He would even read my mail and search through my belongings.

I stuck to my guns and moved house – tried to stand up to him – but back then it felt so difficult to do; it felt like he had got into my head, had the power over me I couldn't understand.

Second Home Memories

When I moved into my second home, I was so happy. The kids seemed relaxed and the place was peaceful, just like I knew it would be. I had the chance to do the right thing and find happiness, and the kids loved their new school, which was ten minutes away. People in the area were very friendly and there were lots of nice shops, but because I didn't drive even the corner shops seemed miles away.

The hill I lived on was extremely steep and it was a long walk up it to my house, especially in the snow, rain and heat with bags of food and a buggy.

A few days after the move, he drove up to my home and sat outside, waiting for me to arrive. I began to think: Who am I kidding? I am never going to get away from him.

I was too scared to go to the police because I thought they would think that I was a bad mother for not getting away from the situation and that they would take my children. I didn't want to be in the situation I was in but I didn't know how to begin to get out of it.

I started to crumble. I was unable to resist once he was there, pressuring me, wearing me down mentally by going on and on at me, following me around. I began letting him come round and entertained him. I tried to focus on me and the kids, not letting him draw me back in. I so wanted to have my new start and not let him get back in my life. He kept showing up, taking the kids out in order to get into my good books. I knew that he was doing that for my benefit as he was never the sort of father to take his children out to spend quality time with them; there was always a motive behind it.

While I was living in my second home, money was hard to come by. The benefit money I had for the children was barely enough to buy food for the week, after the rent and bills had been paid, and looking after two children alone was hard and tiring at times. Every couple of days, I would buy two or three bags of food because when I did a big shop for the week I would always run out of something mid-week and end up with nothing.

I was responsible for myself and my children. The idea of running out of money would worry me so I made sure that I spent it carefully. Sometimes, if I had money troubles, I would turn to my family. During these times, he was working, but his idea of giving me help with money would be by throwing £10.00 at me now and again. Generally, I did it all: school uniform, trips, clothes, etc.

He could see that the children needed clothes and shoes but he never lifted a finger to buy them. If he bought the odd thing for them, it would be because he had an 'agenda'. Back then, I constantly made it clear how hard things were and that he needed to pay for his children, but there was always excuses. "I have bills to pay" or "I have no money left." He never liked giving his money to me or the kids; he would rather take us to the shop and buy what we needed if he really had to and keep the change for himself.

Most days, I would get up, wash and feed the kids and then we would walk to Tesco. I would get two or three bags of food and walk back up the hill again. I didn't have enough money to get a bus so, mostly, me and the kids walked. Sometimes, I would have some change and put money on my Oyster card and get a bus home afterwards.

I also needed to make sure that there was enough money for the gas to keep us warm during cold weather and that there were enough meals for a few days.

Abused: Surviving an Abusive Relationship

When I dropped my son off at school during the week, I made use of the stay and play facility at the school. When I had the two of them, I would take them to the park. There were three really nice parks near my home and I used to carry their bikes and scooters, make sandwiches, bring bottles of drinks and spend a few hours there with them.

Every so often, I would visit the local charity shops with the kids, and soon came to realise that they had some really nice things for the children: board games, DVDs, CDS, toys, books. They loved visiting them. One day, I walked in and saw a pink and white wooden baby highchair. It looked brand new and my little girl loved it. It was such a nice feeling to be able to treat them, although we didn't have a lot, but the prices were good: 50p to £1.00 mostly.

My godmother called me one day out of the blue and, during our conversation, she asked me why I was not driving yet. I said, "I have no money, Auntie. I cannot afford all of that." She told me that she would send a cheque for £200 so that I could book some lessons. I was really appreciative of this; it was very generous, but a huge part of me was scared because I didn't have any confidence left.

I had been at home for so long with my children, which played a big part in affecting my confidence, as well as what he had done and was continuing putting me through. I was therefore hoping that learning to drive would help me to get 'myself' back.

However, I didn't believe I could pass my driving test; I had never had any driving lessons before and wasn't sure I would be able to follow it through. I spoke to my parents and they said that they would help me pay for my lessons once the money had run out because I wouldn't be able to afford it on my own. I began lessons with my brother's close friend, who is a driving instructor and has known me from when I was very small. He has taught many members of my family to drive and is very patient.

He had me begin on the back streets near my home. I decided to drive an automatic because I had been advised by my instructor and my family that it was easier. He went through the initial checks and I attempted to move the car forward. The car lurched forward a few times but it wasn't as bad as I had imagined it would be.

As the weeks went on, it got better. I stuck to one or two lessons a week. I also took my theory test, failed it, went back and passed, which really boosted my confidence, making me think that I was half way there. I didn't tell him about my lessons as I knew he would be negative about it.

Whenever I made mistakes during my lessons, I used to wonder if my instructor thought I was stupid and that I was wasting his time. I had become what I feared I would become: paranoid of what everyone was thinking when they looked at me. He made me feel so low, I constantly doubted myself although I knew that my instructor would never think these things about me.

My children's dad had planted the seeds in my mind with the things he would tell me when he put me down. As I improved each week, I started thinking: Maybe I can do this. I didn't fully believe it, but I began having more faith in myself. I had a vision of progression and having something to feel proud of. Soon, life will be much easier for me and the kids, and we won't have to struggle like we have done anymore.

One hot summer's day I had a shower and put on a maxi dress. I was having a driving lesson and was really looking forward to it, feeling brighter in myself. As I was doing my hair, he walked in and stood in the doorway, staring at me.

At first, he didn't say a word while he was watching me doing my hair and looking me up and down, but then his facial expression changed and he said, "So, why are you wearing that?" I looked at my clothes and then looked at him. "What's the problem?" I replied. "Why are you getting so dressed up to go on a driving lesson? Are you fucking him?" I turned around and stared at him, and then I turned back and continued doing my hair. I said, "I am not even going to validate that with an answer."

I thought that he was disgusting, that he had no respect and that for him to speak to me like that was out of order. However, instead of letting him spoil my day – which was his plan – I ignored him.

Me looking more happy and not showing an interest in his nonsense was definitely bothering him. He was used to me sitting at home, feeling low; same routine. He liked to be in control.

"Why are you driving an automatic anyway? Only old people drive automatics! You call driving an automatic driving? You and your family are fucking idiots!"

I walked in and out of the room and we barely spoke, which was like most days. He stood back to scrutinise me with as though I was doing something wrong. He was so jealous of me doing my driving lessons; he could see I was happier since I had started them. I didn't care, and refused to let him get to me. I just continued focusing on what I was doing. I was concentrating on me.

I really wanted to be happy and not find it hard to get by. Moving house to get away from him was good because I began to feel happy, and when I looked in the mirror I started to feel confident.

I didn't wake up with that darkness inside me but, despite that, I was anxious with him harassing me.

One night, I came home and the house was in darkness. I had had a bad vibe the entire day before I had even got home but I tried to ignore it. I went into my son's bedroom, switched the light on and found him hiding behind the wardrobe on his knees, staring at me. I screamed as an immediate reaction.

He got up calmly and said, "What the f*** are you screaming for?" He walked straight past me; that frightened me even more because he was behaving calmly. He followed me into the kitchen, knocked what I was holding out of my hands, came up really close to me, with

36

his nose touching mine, and whispered: "We are going to party tonight! Yep, we are going to party tonight! Yep, we are going to dance tonight!"

All the time he had a horrible grimace on his face and spoke to me through gritted teeth. All of this because he wanted me to give him another chance. In his mind, begging wasn't working as well as it used to, so threatening, intimidating behaviour was his next option.

The phone then rang. "Hello," he says in a happy, upbeat voice. "How you doing?" He spent the majority of this phone call laughing loudly and behaving normally. I'm sure that the person on the other end had no clue regarding what was really happening.

I stood there shaking and thinking what to do next. I unlocked the window and, the first opportunity I got, ran away. I called the police but by the time they got to my home he was gone. The officers advised me to stay with a friend that night and, the following morning, when I went back, I looked through the letterbox and saw him walking around my home.

I would have my friends and family constantly worrying – feeling disappointed I was allowing him to do this to me –

but I felt stuck in a rut and didn't know how to find the strength to change it all.

I would visit my family, wearing polo-necked jumpers and long-sleeved tops to hide the scratches and bruises. For every mark I had, he had an excuse to make it sound justified in his mind. "Melanie marks easily." "If your hand wasn't in the way, my nail wouldn't have scratched you." "It was an accident."

Later on – much later on – he bragged that he had come in while I was sleeping in my first home and had searched my email, calendar, etc. "I knew where you were moving to the entire time."

A Random Day

I had a photo on my wall, near to my bed, of me and my brother. Another pick on Melanie day. Can't remember what it was all about. He told me to stand still and not move.

He didn't like the fact that I was leaning back as he was speaking so he told me to stand up and when I was ready to answer I must let him know. I ignored him and rolled my eyes. He enjoyed speaking to me as though I was one of the children. I stared at this photo of me and my brother. He said, "Yeah, you keep staring at that photo. You love your family more than me anyway."

I was so sick of him I didn't even answer. With that, he snatched the photo off the wall and tore it ever so slowly in front of my face into two pieces. While he was tearing it up, he had a smirk on his face. I laughed and kept smiling because he liked it when I showed emotion or looked remotely upset. He liked knowing his actions affected me because it made him feel powerful over me.

"If you leave me I will kill myself."

"I couldn't cope without you."

"Please don't leave me!"

"I love you."

"I will go and kill myself right now if you walk away!"

"Give me another chance."

I heard this so many times after the abuse that I had lost count!

My Pain

I sat there on my bed. To my left was a large pile of hair; I looked to my right where the second pile was. I remember tears streaming down my arm, dripping on to my hair, shaking and feeling like nothing.

I had made a really nice potato salad but he was not talking to me over something trivial again. It never had to be major things for him to sulk, ignore me and behave nastily towards me. I walked past him, after having ignored him for some time, and said, "If you fancy some potato salad, it's on the side."

I didn't really care if he was hungry or not but, because I didn't want to listen to him speaking, I offered him the food. I didn't wait for a reply; I just went straight to bed to relax and watch TV. He followed me into my room.

"How dare you ask me that? Am I an idiot? You know I don't eat potato salad!   You   do   it   on purpose? Why are you pretending you didn't know? All the time you've known me have I ever eaten that?"

He repeated this over and over and over again. Here we go! He's going to start again. I can feel it coming!

I replied, "I don't want to hear it anymore. Leave me alone."

He turned the TV off, pulled the blanket off my body, jumped on top of me and began choking me while pinning my arms underneath his knees. I remember him sweating like mad. "Now I'm going to ask you some questions and you better think carefully before you answer them." He squeezed my throat so hard my heart started racing like mad.

He made me sit upright. "Get up!"

I stood up and he used one hand to repeatedly push me in my chest back into a sitting position. That day, I was wearing my hair down. He grabbed it tightly and yanked my head from side to side. I actually felt it when it pulled away from my scalp, although, surprisingly, I didn't actually feel any pain as it came away. He repeated this again at the front of my head and then continued abusing me mentally and physically for a good while.

Afterwards, he kept apologising on his knees, crying his eyes out. "If I lose you I will die! Please forgive me."

He then tried to be intimate with me. When I told him not to touch me or come anywhere near me, he walked away.

If I had slept with him, in his mind that would mean I forgave him. Then he would feel better about what he had just done.

This act of violence was completely off the scale. I was extremely low; I had nothing left in me as far as self-worth was concerned. I know that to allow someone to do this to me and do nothing is difficult for people who haven't been in this situation to understand. He made his behaviour normal, he manipulated me, he wore me down mentally. When you're worn down emotionally, you have no fight in you to make productive life-changing decisions.

The following day, I took a wide-toothed comb and went through my hair in sections. Two handfuls came out. I sat in front of the mirror and cried for the longest time while he slept. When he woke up, he saw all the hair and cried, telling me over and over:

"I'm sorry! I'm so sorry! I didn't mean for this to happen. I love you. Please! I'm going to get help! I will cut off all my hair if it makes you feel better."

Unbelievable!

However, most of the time when the abuse was taking place he showed no compassion or remorse. "It's your fault. If you didn't speak to me like that I wouldn't have got angry!"

Then, afterwards, "Sorry" would follow; it always did follow! He was good at pretending. Good at making me and others think he really loved me and cared about me but deep down he believed I deserved it; he saw nothing wrong with himself.

Since that day, every time I have my hair done at the hairdressers, when I have the middle section blow-dried, the heat rushes straight to my toes because the hair follicles have been permanently damaged. It's really hard when I'm getting on with my life to be reminded of the pain he caused me.

I continued to smile in front of everyone I knew, behaving as though all was fine. However, I did speak to my close friend about it and she kept telling me to go to the police. She was constantly worried for me and the kids' safety when we were with him. I blanked it all out because it was all too painful to face. The most painful part was failing my babies. Blanking it out was my way of getting through it all. I continued with my driving lessons; I had to have something to look forward to. Something good.

Miscarriage

For a long while after he had pulled out my hair, he began to improve in his behaviour. However, he would still isolate me from certain people but he would do it by telling me things to put me off them; he was good at manipulating. He did it so well to the point where you couldn't see it happening, and he could do it with the simplest of things, for example, I would notice his cousin would barely say hello when seeing me with him. He wasn't nasty about it, but he would do everything to avoid me. When I mentioned it to him, he would say, "I don't know what his problem is. I will speak to him. Maybe it's because me and him haven't really been talking, but I'm not letting him or no one treat you this way." Only later did I find out that he didn't like his cousin speaking to me. Apparently, he made such an issue about it that most of his cousins stayed away because of how he behaved.

The violence settled and things were better.

Oh my Lord, I'm pregnant again! This was the last thing I wanted with someone like him. I felt really unhappy but was trying so hard to make myself think I was happy.

I knew deep down that I couldn't trust him. I knew that he would let me down again and that now that I was pregnant he was going to start being abusive again. What had I done? Why wasn't I more careful? It was bad enough that the children I already had suffered; I didn't want another child to go through that. These were all the things I was thinking during this time.

Knowing what my children had suffered emotionally was something I had to blank out because I couldn't take that guilt. I love my children and, inside, because I was so weak, I felt like I was failing them. I wanted them to grow up around love, happiness and laughter, as I did.

When it was me and the kids, we were happy and relaxed. My good friend used to always say to me, "Your home is supposed to be your haven, your sanctuary, the one place you have peace of mind." As soon as he was around, the atmosphere changed.

Sometimes, when he was nice and relaxed, I used to wish it could last forever. When he began to ill-treat me, I found I didn't bother to yearn for it because I knew it wouldn't last long. He was like the weather: his mood and personality would change on at least five occasions during a single day.

I sat down in shock when I told him I was pregnant. I looked, according to him, like someone had died. He looked really upset because he couldn't understand why I wasn't happy and excited by this.

Twelve weeks passed. One day, I was at home, and he started shouting at me for something. I was leaning down to sort out some magazines when he came over, stood up in front of me and said, repeatedly, "I'm talking to you, Melanie. Can you hear me talking to you? I'm talking to you."

I felt my heart racing because I knew that that was normally how he would approach me before he became violent. I didn't want to run the risk of him hurting me while I was carrying a baby so I put my shoes on and ran out of the door. I went straight to my friend's house, who lived five minutes away. I sat on her settee and poured my heart out to her. I remember feeling very emotional and as I finished speaking I began to bleed. When I got home, as I opened the door, he wanted to argue, argue, argue. He followed me into every room, going on and on like he always did. I said, "I'm bleeding. Please just leave me alone."

He went quiet for moment and then said, "Melanie, you need to go to the hospital. Why won't you go?"

I said: "Because I'm scared of what they will say."

He went straight into my bathroom and cried, then came out and called for an ambulance. When the ambulance men arrived, he acted like the concerned, devoted, loving partner, fussing over me, questioning the ambulance men on why this was happening. "I'm leaving now, kids. Kiss mummy!" Two lovely kisses to give me strength.

He stood there waiting for me to hug him. I could tell because he put on his 'feel sorry for me' face. I hugged him with no warmth; it was like a pat on the back sort of hug. I felt my skin crawl because I couldn't bear to be near him but, again, because I wanted to avoid his mouth later, I just did it quickly so that I wouldn't suffer later. He wanted me to make his conscience better but I wasn't going to be a part of it.

It was so early in my pregnancy that I had to wait until the following morning to be seen. That was the hardest night of my life. I knew that my baby was gone. I watched the nurse as she examined me and I remember I kept watching her reaction with my heart racing. She said, "I'm sorry,

47

there's no heartbeat." They called him in to be with me. I had to speak to the doctor about my options. He kicked off, saying, "We don't want to discuss it now. I need to look after my girl."

He behaved so badly that the lady asked me if she could speak to me alone. I couldn't take the stress, so I said no. I knew he was coming back to mine later, and I would only have to listen to his mouth. I found that I would surrender to anything to not hear his mouth; when he would start he would repeat himself over and over again until I felt like I was going crazy.

He was always mean with his money but, having been just told that my baby had died, feeling weaker than I had ever felt and then having to take two buses home was awful, especially when he told me he had money. I had to put on a brave face for my children, think about their dinner and bath time.

A lot of resentment and anger was building inside me as the days went by but I was so weak and vulnerable that I didn't fully realise it. I was partly leaning on him with being so low but also resenting him because I felt that it was all his fault. When we argued, he constantly drummed it into my head that it was my fault because I never wanted the baby to begin with. He told me that I was the one who had decided to have the miscarriage at home. When the miscarriage started, I stood in the shower, crying, and he came in and asked me in a sickly sweet voice, "Do you feel guilty?"

I knew what he meant but I didn't answer him because I couldn't take any more emotionally. He chose to say that to me at the lowest point in my life. It wasn't my fault; I believe it was his. He knew it was. If he hadn't stressed me out, it never would have happened. To make himself feel better – as always – he would break me down mentally.

A few nights later, I woke up in the middle of the night with a horrific pain. I don't believe I have felt a pain like that in all my life. I called 999 but they couldn't do anything for me. The miscarriage had taken effect and I had to let my body do its work. I don't know what I would have done without my hot water bottle that night; it was as bad as being in actual labour.

I had no one to comfort me or hold my hand. While I spoke with the ambulance lady over the phone, he came into my room, complaining that I hadn't told tell him that I wanted to call them. I didn't answer him. While I was crying and rocking back and forth with the phone in my hand he said, "Don't make so much noise! You're going to wake up the kids!"

A few days later, it was my son's birthday. During this time, the miscarriage was still taking place. I was supposed to be resting. He came round and lay in my bed, complaining he had no money, his baby had died and he was depressed. I got the children ready and, as we went to leave, he lay there sulking. I didn't even hear him wish his son a happy birthday. I took the children to my parents to collect my son's birthday money, and then I took him to Pizza Hut with a friend. I couldn't bear the thought of keeping him home all day. I was very weak and in a lot of pain but I wanted him to enjoy his special day.

The following day, he came round again. That morning, I barely exchanged two words with him. He went and lay down on my bed again. There was no food in the house so I got the children ready and we went shopping. The three of us walked back up the hill with the shopping; my son helping me carry some of the bags because I couldn't manage them. My son was 7 years old at the time.

I rang my close friend, who I knew through him, and told her about how I had lost the baby and how I blamed him, but I didn't tell her the rest at the time because I felt so embarrassed. She said, "Mel, don't worry. Just keep concentrating on you. You will get there. Concentrate on yourself and you will do what needs to be done soon."

That day, I carried the baby's scan picture with me; it made me feel close to the baby. Before I left, I told him how fed up I was with his lack of support. When I returned, he backed me up to the wall in my son's bedroom and told me to give him the scan picture. "Who gave you permission to take the picture that should have been where I left it?" He screamed at me, behaving crazily: "Give it to me now! I want it now! I'm not waiting. I ain't moving till I get it!" His nose was touching mine. "You better give it to me now. I need it for strength. How dare you take it from me like that! I could have killed myself. That would have been your fault."

Bad Memories while Miscarrying

He choked me, slapped me, pushed me into furniture repeatedly, told me that it was my fault and that I had depression. He slapped me so hard I felt dizzy, and then he locked me in the bedroom. He would repeat what he was angry about over and over. From the other side of the locked door he would ask me questions like:

"Why do you cause so many problems?"

"I want to know why you are treating me like a c***!"

"You are not leaving this room until I get a decent explanation!"

"Don't worry, I have all day. Doesn't bother me."

"Yeah, you keep giving me attitude."

"My baby is dead because of you."

This would go on and on for hours.

In the room, he would say things like:

"Why have you caused all of this?"

"You never wanted my baby!"

"You feel guilty deep down, don't you?"

"If you wanted this baby to begin with, this never would have happened."

"You want me to hate you. Well, guess what, I do. I can't stand you."

I even remember pretending I was having pain and asking him to call the ambulance so that I could get away from him, and he refused.

The Unforgivable

One night, I spent the evening with his parents. I had dinner with the children, and his dad offered to drop me home. While he was driving, he mentioned my miscarriage and the fact that he had heard about it. He also mentioned that he was worried about me as to how I coped because he knew his son did nothing to help me.

I told him about how the miscarriage had happened. He said, "Your pain goes straight through me," then went quiet. He kept nodding his head and then said to me, "Would you like to get away?" I replied, "Yeah." He added, "I mean, away from it all. If you had the chance, would you?" I replied, "Definitely, with what I've been through. Who wouldn't?" He was acting concerned and said, "You need rest; it takes a long time for a woman to recover from a miscarriage."

We arrived at my house and I stepped out of the car and went through the front door with the children ahead of me. His father walked in behind me, and I went to put my bags down. I was going to say my goodbyes but he said, "Take their coats off and sort them out 'cos I want to talk to you."

So I took their coats off and got them ready for bed, used the bathroom and came out. When I came out towards the front door where he was standing he told me to close the living room door behind me. I figured at this point that he had something personal to discuss with me about his son.

He put his hand around my waist and said, "Would you like me to take you away, just you and me?" I said, "What are you talking about?"

I pulled his hand away and began to feel uncomfortable so I backed away from him. However, because I trusted him so much it still wasn't clicking in my mind, maybe because it was so unbelievable. He then tried to hug me. As I resisted, he tried to put one of his hands under my top. I quickly grabbed his hand and shouted, "What are you doing?"

I remember standing there staring at him in utter shock and disbelief. I fully understood what he was up to, and the fact that he had crossed the line and tried to violate me was devastating. He looked at me and said, "Oh, you're surprised, aren't you?"

I was still staring at him in shock. "Yeah, you're shocked, I know." Then he changed the subject and began talking about something else. I interrupted him, and said, "Why did you do that?" He ignored me but I cut him off and said, "No! What you just did, why did you do that?"

He replied, "I'm sorry," looking rather embarrassed and uncomfortable. "I'm really sorry. You're shocked. Okay, I'm going to go." At that point, he opened the door behind him and quickly left.

I stood there, trying to make sense of what had just happened, then picked up the phone and called my mum. She said, "Don't say anything. If he ever does it again, then tell but until then leave it. This will affect a lot of people. The man is lost and confused."

I was so shocked when she said this because I figured that she would have advised me to speak up, but, as I said at the beginning of this book, his family and my family had known one another before me and him had met each other. So, with the situation as it stood, it would be like opening up a can of worms. I was against her advice, but I promised her I would keep quiet.

Mum then said, "This will send your young man over the edge. He already has a lot of unresolved issues. He's already messed up. Something bad could go down from this and if it gets out of hand, I'm not in the country. What will my friends say if they knew what he did?"

The following day was his wife's birthday. A meal had been arranged for her. Her son – my partner – my kids and I were due to attend that evening. I went to my friend's home early that morning and she told me to speak to his father. She agreed that I should say something. I called him, and he told me that he was on his way to my home with my partner's cousin. He was talking normally and said he would speak to me in a while.

When I went back home, his father came in to pick him up as they were going to do a job for someone. When no one was looking, he stood near me and said, "You just don't understand. Your pain goes straight through me. Yeah, we will talk."

I felt really afraid because, from his behaviour, I didn't trust him anymore. I felt as though I didn't know what he was capable of doing anymore, and was uncomfortable and disgusted by him and the whole situation. I left to take my children to the park, called my mum, and she asked if I had kept my promise. I told her I had. She advised me to speak to his dad and let him know that I didn't appreciate his indiscretion and that, if it happened again, I would not hesitate to tell his son and everyone else.

I still didn't agree with the plan so she put my dad on the line. He also agreed with her and said, "I know you can't see what we are saying now, but we are older and wiser. Believe us, this is the best way to handle it."

My worry was that if he tried to take advantage again and decided to speak up and mention that this had happened before, no one would believe me. I had a while to think and, against my wishes, decided to follow my parents' advice. I was hoping that, later on, I would see what they were trying to tell me. I also decided to record any further conversations between me and his dad in case anything further happened.

When I got back from the park, my partner and his father were at my home. At this point, I felt angry towards his dad because going over the situation over and over again was upsetting me more and more, especially as I wanted to say something so badly. I wasn't speaking to his son at this time – as always – so when I walked in and angrily looked at the two of them, my partner didn't think anything of it.

His father came straight to my bedroom and said, "Come with me, Mel. I'm going to take you for a drive so we can talk."

He was in the kitchen and so his dad said to him in front of me, "I'm going to have a chat with Mel. I won't be long." He made it out as though he was going to speak to me about my and his son's problems, so everything had been planned out nicely by him. As I went to get into the car, I set my Blackberry – which was in my pocket – to record. He confessed to everything. I asked him how he could do such a thing. He kept saying sorry and that it would never happen again. I told him that I felt guilty even though I'd done nothing wrong, but keeping quiet made me feel bad. He begged me not to say anything. "Please act natural. Please don't be scared of me. I won't let you down. Please don't say anything!"

I still have the recording because I still do not trust him.

I went to the birthday celebrations as planned. When I was sitting at the table, my older sister and my mum and dad called me to see if everything was okay.

From that day onwards, I have kept my distance. In some ways, I regret not speaking, because I did nothing wrong and, on top of the abuse I had already endured, I don't feel I should have let this go. Back then, I was disrespected, violated, humiliated in every way, shape and form; not only by him but by his family.

At this point, I knew I had to get myself and my children away from people like this. Something inside of me definitely felt different. I knew I would soon be at the stage to fully make that break but I still wasn't ready. I never had any hope before this because I had been broken down emotionally but I knew things would be better for me soon.

Major Life Lesson

After being in South Croydon for two years, I decided to try and get a bigger property through Home Swapper, but had no joy for months. I remember doing my own search as the automated system was taking far too long.

One day, I saw a house online. When I viewed the pictures, I thought, "I can never get that". The kitchen was huge, and the whole house was nicely decorated with laminated floors and a large garden. It was a three-bedroomed property in Upper Norwood. In truth, I wanted something the same size in South Croydon but, loving it so much, I didn't care; didn't think I would have any luck as I only had a maisonette. Either way, I gave the lady a call and she asked me for details about my home. She told me that, unfortunately, she wanted a living room and dining room that were separate from one another.

After I had said my goodbyes and hung up, a few minutes later she called me, saying that she had viewed a property in Catford and that she wanted it but the couple she was swapping with wanted something smaller. She gave me their contact details. It was worth a try! I called and arranged for them to come round to view my home. They wanted it! I really couldn't believe my luck. All parties agreed and we did a three-way swap.

My family helped me move and settle in. During this time, my children were still going to school in South Croydon, so we would get up at 6.00 a.m. and leave at 7.15 to get the 7.30 bus. We had to take two or three buses to get to their school in the morning. After dropping them off, I had driving lessons, followed by trying to get back to let the decorator in, food shopping and unpacking.

I had to leave my home at 1.45 in the afternoon to get to the school for 3 o'clock to collect the children, so it didn't leave me a lot of time to get much done. I put the children's names down on the waiting list for a school closer to home but in the meantime I didn't want them to miss out on their education.

I felt very guilty back then, having them get up so early. I asked them how they were feeling and if they were happy going to this school. They said that they loved it and didn't really want to move as they had made friends and were settled.

I wanted to work, and needed to provide for my children. Being a single mother, it was difficult but I had no money coming in. My little girl was now older so I started looking for work.

I managed to find myself a part-time job at a new nursery around the corner from the kids' school. The job was to run the after school club, and so I would be able to collect my children and have them with me.

At the interview, I gave the manager lots of ideas for after school activities and she seemed impressed. A few days later, after doing a trial day, she called to offer me the job. We wanted for nothing with me getting this job.

I would cook during the day and bring the kids' dinner with me, so, when I finished work at 6.00 p.m., on the long bus journey home they could have a decent dinner. If I had waited to get them home to have dinner it would have been a long wait for them because every evening it took an hour and a half to get home. By the time they got home, they would be exhausted, poor things.

There was still no news about a school in my area so I kept going with this arrangement although it was hard on the kids because I needed the money to feed them and pay my bills. When the snow fell, and we were fed up, I kept telling them, "Don't worry, things will be better for us soon. It's just for a while, and mummy will be driving soon."

I thought I was happy. When I had a disagreement with him, he was gentle and calm. He would say, "I will leave you a while. I hope you will speak to me when I come back because I don't want to argue with you. I don't want that old life. I want things to be different this time around. I don't want to control you or bully you in any way. I love you and I'm going to prove myself so you can trust me again."

Many times, I would observe his reactions after situations to see how he responded. He never failed me. I sat and had talks with him about my resentment, also about the fact that we had no friendship due to his old behaviour. He took everything on board and would call me and speak to me for long periods of time or come round and take the children out to spend quality time with them. Previously, it had seemed to be a burden for him, and you could always tell he didn't really want to do it. Now, he looked content and happy spending time with them, and less like he was babysitting. He was helpful, and made it clear that he wanted to start stepping up as a father and a partner, if I would have him. During all of this, I continued with my driving lessons.

Changed Man

"I'm going to church," he says. "I'm spending time with my children." "I'm calm," he says. "When I get angry, I walk away. I want to be a better person. I've done a lot to you. Now, finally, I acknowledge it. I just need God to help me through."

I spent a long time separated from him, and began to feel more relaxed. I wasn't where I fully wanted to be but I gained enough strength during this time to say to myself: "If he touches me again I will not tolerate it". I started to see what normality felt like again, day to day life, having peace of mind and no grief. Inside, I felt that dark cloud over me lifting day by day, feeling stress free, waking up every day not feeling anxious, exhausted and unhappy.

Deep down, however, I felt as though he was still in my head. I knew this because I still allowed him to call, questioning me and crying. I still allowed him to play his mind games with me and do nothing. The only difference was that there was no violence. Physical violence, I mean.

Sometime afterwards, I found that I was pregnant again. No grief, and no headache!

He was treating me better than he had ever treated me. However, deep down, when he kept trying to prove that he had changed, I guess I knew he hadn't. In the back off my mind, I knew it but ignored it and told myself that he was finally everything I wanted him to be but I knew it didn't feel right.

He was never going to be anything else than what he had always been, but at that time he had me convinced for a long while with his 'I've turned over a new leaf' routine.

However, things slowly began to crumble. My feelings were fading slowly, and I was unable to keep up with housework because my health was bad. He didn't lift a finger to help me; he never helped with the kids or money, and everything was back to how it was. I was going nonstop from 6.00 a.m. until 10. 00 or 11.00 p.m. Being pregnant and unwell was killing me. I felt so low that I could barely walk with the pain every week. There was something wrong.

Despite it all, I continued with my driving lessons. I pushed and pushed but had to take time of work when I was really unwell. The doctor signed me off to take some rest but I still kept going because I didn't want to lose my job. There were even times when, because the kids and I had to leave so early, the message to say that school had been cancelled wouldn't come through until we were nearly there. I would then have to travel all the way back and stay at home because I wasn't allowed to bring them to work and had no one to help me with them.

In the end, my manager sacked me. I started panicking. I had a baby on the way, two children to feed, and bills to pay. On the other hand, I felt relieved because my body couldn't keep going anymore.

Me losing my job didn't change his attitude; he was still carefree and unhelpful.

When he was around, I spent most of my time ignoring him. I went to Ikea and saw a cot, wardrobe and changing table for the bargain price of £120. I had nothing for the coming baby and wanted to get organised. He rang me as I left the shop and asked me where I was. I told him about the deal but in my own mind I had planned to pay for it alone, as I normally did. He told me he would give me the money for it. Two weeks later, he got the money but, before he gave me it, he asked to see the receipt. I was so annoyed that I told him to keep his money. He was so disrespectful, considering he did nothing else, and gave me nothing for his children.

At five months pregnant, one morning while the children were waiting in their coats to go to school, he started shouting at me in front of them over something trivial. He followed me into the kitchen, filled a long glass of water and threw it all over me. The children stood at the kitchen door watching the entire thing. He continued shouting in my face, and then told the children to go to their rooms.

He's Back!

As soon as the children left the room, he slammed the kitchen door, ran towards me, grabbed me from behind and put his arm around my neck, squeezing my throat as tightly as he could. I was unable to breathe for a long while. While I was struggling and trying to release his hands, I fell to my knees on the kitchen floor. He pushed his whole weight on to my back, which forced me to lie flat. My stomach was pressing into the kitchen floor while he was lying on my back with his hands still around my neck. I thought, "He's going to kill me and this baby I'm carrying if I stay in this situation a moment longer". I remember him holding my neck for so long that I began to lose the urge to fight.

He called my daughter from upstairs, sat her on his knee and asked her who was arguing: mummy or daddy. Was daddy trying to speak to mummy, and did mummy listen? She looked confused and unsure of what to say. He sent her back upstairs.

I told him that the children needed to eat their breakfast. He screamed in my face, constantly ignoring me. "I don't care! You care more about everything else than me and what's happening here!" He then grabbed me, pushed me around the kitchen, getting in my face. "See, even my children can see what you are like! How sad is that? I am glad they can see what you're like."

I told him that I needed to go to the bathroom because I thought I was bleeding. He told to me check myself right there. "You ain't going nowhere!"

He shouted and shouted for the longest time. I switched off in order to get through it. As I attempted to leave the room to use the bathroom, he followed me upstairs and stood outside the bathroom door. When he heard the toilet flush, he pushed the door open, grabbed me and then shoved me back down the stairs as I started walking down them.

As I walked back into the kitchen, he picked up my mobile phone as it started ringing, chucked it into the living room, then instantly slammed the door. He began shouting abuse at me all over again. I told him that I needed to call the children's school to report their absence. "Where is my phone?" He refused to tell me. "The children haven't eaten." He shouted for ages while the children were upstairs, "I need to give them something to eat." He lit himself a cigarette and put some bread in the toaster. When it was ready, he called our son, who was 9 at the time. He cracked open the kitchen door, handed him the plate through the gap and told him to share it with his sister. He then started to calm down. His expression said that he was now unsure of what I would do.

I looked for my phone and, when I had found it, dialled the children's school. I had left him in the room, and closed the door, but he stood there watching me. Before the call connected, he opened the door and said to me, "They are my children. I'm their dad and I will call them myself."

"Hello?"

"Yes, hello. I am calling in regard to my children. As you are aware, my partner is pregnant and she is under the weather today. I am going to take the day off from work. It's my duty to look after her." After he was asked why my daughter was not attending, he replied, "Oh, yeah, and she is unwell also so I am going to keep them home."

I stood at the door with my coat on and he blocked my way. "Where are you going?" "To get milk." "What for?" "Because I am pregnant and you have not let me eat all morning." "Have something else." "There's no food here. I need to eat!"

He went on and on for a while until he got bored and moved out of the way so that I could leave. As soon as the door opened, I started to hurry, opened the gate and walked down the road.

Suddenly, I stopped walking and – I remember this moment so well –stood still for a few moments when it hit me:

What are you doing, Mel? What on earth have you been doing?

I refer to this moment as having been fast asleep for fifteen years and then waking up. I finally got it!

I continued to walk, and started to smile. God had answered my prayers. I knew what I needed to do now!

My cup had overflowed. People always said to me, "Mel, one day you will wake up to it all and say, 'I've had enough'." I never believed that would happen to me – only the people around me believed. I can honestly say, I couldn't wait to get to this place because I so wanted to be happy and get away from him.

I wanted this baby I was carrying to have a fresh start in life: my baby doesn't deserve this sort of start; my children don't deserve this life anymore; I don't deserve to be treated this way. If he can do this and I'm pregnant, what next?

I love my children and I chose them. It's my job to protect them and set an example for them. They should have the childhood I had.

I went straight to the police station and reported him. I watched from a police car while they arrested him. I couldn't wait for it to be over and could barely feel my legs as I tried to lift myself out of the police car. The officer helped me as my stomach kept contracting with the stress and anxiety of it all.

The police also asked me to go to the hospital to be checked over. However, I knew that once I got away from him I would be okay.

When I got to the door, my children were there waiting for me. I was so worried about them because I no longer knew what he was capable of, so seeing that they were okay made me feel a lot better. I just wanted to be there for them because I knew they were feeling it so much with all that had happened, and I wanted them to know that they had one parent there for them.

That same evening, his brother, father and uncle came to my home uninvited, arguing among themselves. His brother behaved aggressively. Just like him. Manipulative, just like him. That night, I made my feelings clear to his brother, not only in regards to his behaviour in my home but also in that he had known his brother abused me and had done nothing about it.

I finally stood up to all of them. They had all been witness to the mental and physical bullying, but they were happy so long as they didn't have him to deal with. They always – especially his mother – encouraged me to stay with him even when they knew what he was doing to me. None of them wanted to deal with him.

Humiliation Again

A few weeks later, I found out from the hospital that he had given me a STD infection, which could cause my baby to be born prematurely or with a low birth weight. I had had it for some time during the pregnancy but hadn't been aware of it. To know that I was carrying his baby and that he could still be so heartless as to put the baby at risk like that resulted in me feeling absolutely nothing for him. I didn't love him anymore, so nothing he did could hurt me.

I was thankful that it was something that could be cured. My baby was still healthy, despite the infection and the stress he had caused me.

The hospital sent me to an STD clinic. I asked if I could see my GP instead but the nurse said I could not get my medication from the doctor's surgery.

When I walked, in I used my coat to cover my stomach. I rested my bag in front of me the entire time and sat in the corner so as not to draw attention to myself. I had done nothing wrong or to be ashamed of but, being in a place like that and being pregnant made me feel like the lowest thing on earth.

"If I didn't have to be here I wouldn't be". "Would people in here think I didn't come from a respectable family home?" I had to keep reminding myself of the importance of why I had to be there. Again, I had done nothing to be ashamed of, but it was so humiliating. I felt violated.

During this time, I had no electricity or food so I had to stay with a close friend that night. Things were like this for at least two months. I always made sure my children had breakfast, lunch and dinner at all times. I tried to sell my things so that I could find money to feed my children, take them to school and buy snacks for them.

I sold most of my clothes and possessions to feed my children and myself. There were nights when there wasn't enough to go round so I would feed my children, put them to bed and go to bed hungry. The worst period was going hungry for two days. Walking up and down, pregnant and hungry, was hard. I just kept thinking that things were going to get better; it wouldn't be like this forever.

I then had to go to King's College Hospital to be seen by a midwife due to the bleeding and pain. I was regularly in and out of hospital with this sort of problem during my pregnancy.

As I sat down in the waiting room, I felt that I was going to faint. The staff had to get me a cup of tea because my body wouldn't stop shaking. I was very hungry and my body wasn't responding well. After being seen, I walked from Kings College Hospital to Brixton and discovered that I had £6.00 in my account that morning.

After I had bought something to eat, I called my mum and told her what I was going through. She told me that she was going to send money from abroad for me and the children. I felt that the decisions I had made had brought me to where I was, so it was no one's problem but my own. But I had to put my pride aside for the sake of my children and my unborn child. I couldn't continue carrying a child and not eating properly.

I had to take out loans and constantly borrow money until the money came through. Along with this, I had rent to pay and a new baby to prepare for. As worried as I felt, I kept telling myself that God would provide; that everything would fall into place.

Not long after, my daughter came down with chickenpox, so I kept them both home from school. I had to keep them both home because I was travelling by bus from Upper

Norwood to South Croydon every day to get them both to school.

That night, I was bleeding and having contractions. My older brother and his partner came to my home and looked after the children. I was worried about going into hospital and being kept in, especially because my little girl wasn't feeling great with the chickenpox and needed me. My brother took me to the hospital to be examined, but that night they discharged me.

The following morning, I had a social worker come to see me, which was something I used to always fear because of the lifestyle I used to live. She was really nice and supportive. I remember my good friend constantly asking me, "Why won't you let them help you?" I used to think that I would be in some kind of trouble, maybe because I was letting him bully me and not having a voice. Her words were always, "You are the victim. You have done nothing wrong!"

When you're in the situation, you can't see this. It's the fear of the unknown. You feel like the authorities will look at you as though you're a bad mother because you're accepting the situation, but the truth of the matter is that, when you live in madness for so long, you feel scared. Can my life be any different than what it is? Will I ever be happy?

The domestic violence organisation, Gaia, has been amazing. They have provided me with extra security in my home to make me feel safer, and I will be starting counselling soon.

I received a letter stating that he had pleaded not guilty to what he had done. He had no idea what he had put me and my children through, and he never will. I decided that I was not going to let him get away with what he had done. I knew it was going to add more stress to my health, being eight months pregnant, but I decided to go to court and give evidence against him.

I didn't want anyone with me. I felt strong enough to go alone and do what I had to do. My brother decided he wanted to come with me for support as I shouldn't go through this alone. To be so late in my pregnancy and due at any moment, to give evidence and be put through that sort of stress was horrible. The evidence was there for all to see but he still refused to take responsibility.

Judgement Day

When we arrived at the court, my brother and I were notified that he had sacked his solicitor and had decided to represent himself. I guess he figured that I wouldn't show. His solicitor most probably told him to plead guilty but he refused. He had been advised that it would be in his interest to have a representative but he refused and decided to represent himself. He doesn't have a law degree, he didn't know what he's doing, he was making this worse for himself.

People said to me that someone who decides to represent themselves has 'lost the plot'. That he had indeed! He figured: "I have this under control because I'm in her head. I can deal with her myself".

It had to be explained to him that he couldn't speak to me directly in court. He wasn't allowed to question me himself, but he had to have someone speak on his behalf, so he had a new solicitor, who he had never met and who barely knew the case, to represent him.

When I entered the courtroom, a screen that I had requested had been put up so that I wouldn't have to see him. This made me feel so much better. I walked into the booth to give evidence against him.

Going over the story again wasn't nice. Afterwards, he took his new solicitor out of the room three times during the hearing to give her information to try and manipulate me.

I think the realisation hit him that he had lost me for good, so he decided to try and set me up for fraud. If he was successful, my punishment would be for me to lose everything, as he had. His objective was to make me believe that he had something on me to make it look as though I was lying. He wanted me to fold under the pressure, to plant fear in my mind that the judge wouldn't believe me, so he invented a few things to try and break me down.

"Is it true, Miss Clarke, that Mr Kennedy was living in your council property and you didn't declare it?"

"Is it true that you told Corinne Hartland (my friend/his cousin's wife) the real versions of events that took place on the day of the attack?"

"You are really the aggressive one, aren't you?"

He tried to make me think that anyone who knew the two of us was willing to give evidence against me to say that I was lying, and that we had been seen out together as a happy family, etc.

On this day in court it wasn't about being found guilty or not guilty; this was a whole lot more profound than that. For him, he wanted to show me: "Even in the courtroom, I can still have you mentally. I can still get in your head. I can still chew you up and spit you out when I manipulate your thoughts".

But he was so busy fixating on ruining me that he couldn't see he was showing the judge and everyone else how bullying, controlling and manipulative he was!

He wanted me to believe that these people were against me and also wanted to get me into trouble to benefit him, which I knew was untrue. He was doing his usual: playing with my mind.

The people he had mentioned were witnesses to the nasty treatment I had endured. They were always supportive of me leaving him because they couldn't believe how badly he treated me and the children.

He didn't once discuss the fact that he assaulted me while I was pregnant. He didn't once mention that he had nearly killed me; he told them that he grabbed my tracksuit top and it grazed my neck. On the day that I reported the attack, photos were taken at the police station. I had red, raw strangulation marks around my neck. In my own words, it looked like someone had thrown a cat at my neck.

I knew what he was doing and so I stuck to what had really happened and did not let him get to me. This wasn't difficult because he could no longer bother, shock or hurt me. Knowing that when I stepped out of the courtroom it would be the end of that chapter of my life was a great feeling. All he did was show everyone what he was really about.

The moment when I did step out of the courtroom, I felt very relieved but when I arrived home I started to bleed again. I knew that it was because of the stress my body was under. During the hearing, I knew he wanted me to fall apart but I stayed strong through it all. I had challenged so many awful things but I got there.

A few weeks later, I received a phone call to say that he had been found guilty.

Being eight months pregnant is very uncomfortable. Since catching the infection, I'd been seeing a midwife every two weeks. My health was bad; the stress had definitely taken its toll on my pregnancy. Despite my health and exhaustion, the kids and I did lots of things together. Seeing them so happy and relaxed made me feel wonderful.

For me, I felt happy and at peace. Knowing that my baby would be born into peaceful surroundings was beyond words. I made this happen. Never knew when I was once in that dark place that this could be so easy. When I looked in the mirror I recognised that person looking back at me. Where had you been?

The Labour

The ambulance did not show and the contractions were constant. I had to get a lift to the hospital that night. I chose to have my baby alone. I did not want a birthing partner. I felt that, with everything that had happened, I needed to do this alone.

That night, when I arrived, I prayed to God to not let my pain be too much for me to bear; make it that me and the baby would be okay. Throughout the pregnancy, I had a constant bad feeling, as if something awful was going to happen.

I pulled hard on the gas and air; kept my pain nice and controlled as long as I could. Forty-one minutes later, my baby boy was here. I felt so much better now that he had arrived but, due to my health problems, I had to stay in hospital for three days. The baby had to be monitored but, luckily, everything was okay.

My cousin collected me from hospital, and my brother took care of my other children. As long as I didn't have my children to worry about, I was okay. When I arrived home from hospital, I grabbed some shopping, cooked and organised everything for my baby.

One week after giving birth, I found out that he had to attend a domestic abuse centre for thirty-six days. When I went to court, I had requested a restraining order to be made against him, which was issued as an indefinite one. I chose a restraining order instead of an injunction because it's more effective and, if breached even once, he could spend five years in prison.

All the things he had put me through flashed through my mind when I received this call. The emotional pain he had caused the children; all the years of abuse I let him get away with and did nothing about. I looked at my baby and thought: "He is going to have a great experience in his childhood now, filled with peace and love around him".

It felt amazing, knowing how happy my children had been, my baby having a fresh start and for knowing that, because of all the years he had got away with hurting me, he now had to face the consequences for his actions.

Brighter Moments

Five weeks after giving birth, I retook my driving test. This was my fourth attempt, and I decided that I was just going to 'go with the flow' and not take it too seriously. Just before I took my test, I was so nervous that I stopped at a chemist and bought some Kalms. I wanted it so badly because I knew that with a new born and my other two children our life would be ten times easier once I could drive.

On my way there I had to think positively and kept telling myself that me passing could happen. Now that I had my life straight, I felt more relaxed and at peace to retake the test. The same lady I had when I had failed the first time was taking me for this one. At that point I had to work hard on my self-confidence and stay focused.

I felt I did well but wasn't sure. "Congratulations, you have passed," she said as she handed me my certificate. As a result of the confidence I used to have that was knocked out of me along the way, at this point I knew I could accomplish things. I just needed to get him out of my life permanently in order for everything else to fall into place.

A few weeks later, with the help of my family, I bought my first car: a Vauxhall Corsa. The kids were very excited. We had struggled for so long and they were able to understand and appreciate what having this car would do for us all. First day out in the new car, the kids and I went food shopping; not having to struggle home with the shopping was my highlight.

Since leaving him, I have felt genuinely happy from the inside out. I used to live a crazy, unsettled life that made me very unhappy. Every day I was stressed out. Back then, I used to suffer with constant aches down one side of my face and bad headaches, which I knew were down to stress and anxiety.

Now, I look forward to each day. It may sound silly to people who haven't been through it, but waking up to peace each day is still very strange for me, but it feels so great to have this peace. I don't have to think what mood he is going to be in. No worry, no fear, no anxiety on a daily basis. Just peace.

I have my family and friends around me whenever I want. I don't have to feel like I need to keep every aspect of my life separate anymore, which is so much more relaxing.

An abusive relationship, whether physical or mental, brings isolation. They like to take you away from all the people who care about you. In doing so, they can manipulate your way of thinking to their way of thinking. This way, you won't leave them when these same people try to talk you into leaving. Then come the excuses you begin to make for your partner when you are challenged by family or friends:

"He has changed."

"He promises he won't do it again."

"He knows if he does I'm leaving next time."

You find yourself defending them and not even knowing why; making excuses in your own mind or to others for their actions, because you're embarrassed to let people know you are letting someone treat you like this and are not doing anything to change it.

Mental Abuse

Have you ever endured this form of mental abuse?

I would look at my phone and he would be calling me. When he received no reply, he would call back straightaway. I would get so tired of him calling that I would put my phone on silent. Later, when I checked my phone, I would see thirty missed calls. He would use this method to wear me down. I used to look at the phone ringing and the door knocking at the same time and think, "Will I ever get away from this life? I am never going to be happy as long as he is around. He will never leave me alone long enough for me to move on with my life".

"Take those leggings off! You look like a tramp!"

"Why are you watching that on TV? Don't you have anything better to do? The TV is a whole load of evil. You watching it says you worship the devil!"

"I don't love you any less because you're not that smart."

"Why haven't you called me all day? I don't know where you are or what you have been doing all day."

"Why are you always talking to your friends on the phone?"

"Why didn't you cancel your phone call and greet me when I came through the door? You care more about your friends than me!"

"Why did you let my friend greet you with a kiss on your cheek? I don't like it."

"Why are you being so friendly to my friends?"

"How come Harmony has fallen and banged her teeth? If she was with me that never would have happened."

"Why are you so stupid?"

"That guy was only looking at you because of the way you are dressed."

"Why don't you pay me any attention?"

He would take my son out and flirt with other woman in front of him and then make him lie about where they had been all day. (I only found this out once I had left him.)

"You're going to see my niece dressed like that? Her boyfriend's going to be there. What are you teaching my niece? You're dressing too provocative to be around her boyfriend."

"Why are you getting so dressed up? Who are you trying to impress?"

He would purposely use words I didn't understand, and then tell me to look them up in the dictionary.

If you didn't agree with what he was saying he would hurl abuse at you and belittle your opinions. "I'm smarter then you'll ever be."

He would make my home untidy, phone his friend to call by and make out when I had left the room that I was untidy and did nothing.

"I'm not watching this s***! If you continue to watch this, I'm going upstairs." For a peaceful life, when I knew he was coming, I would change the channel.

"You can't even help your son with his homework." He would turn to my son and say, "You're stupid like your mother! Why don't you get the homework by now?" This sort of thing would create arguments between me and him.

"Who just called you?" He would listen to every element of my phone call and give me disapproving looks while I was speaking. When I got off the phone, he would try and quiz me. If he didn't get the answers he wanted, he would accuse me of trying to hide something and of behaving suspiciously.

If I ever tried to find the strength to leave him, he would come to my home and ask to spend time with his son. I would let him go with his dad for the day. That way, when he returned, I would have to let him back in.

I booked a holiday in Greece with my friends. He was aware that I had booked it but manipulated me for weeks, nagging and nagging me and even having his mother work on me to wear me down. I ended up caving in and not going.

Why?

Why did I sit down and let him do this to me?

Because I thought I loved him. And, amazingly, despite the fact that he was mentally unwell, underneath all his issues I thought he loved me. He just needed help and then I could be happy being with him. I believed that he didn't mean it deep down; he just needed help with his *anger*, and I could help him be a better him.

However:

You **CAN'T** love someone who tries to harm you!

Someone who wants you to be intimidated by them **CAN'T** love you!

Someone who brings physical violence, physical danger to you **CANT** love you!

The other day, I had a discussion about this love thing. I claimed that I loved him, although he made me so unhappy, but yet I kept going back. Then I figured it out for myself.

When I met him, we had a connection. Despite how controlling he was, I loved him back then. As the years went by and the abuse started, whenever he begged me to stay with him that guy I loved would show up again. I missed that guy! Whenever I saw that guy again, it would tug at my heart strings and draw me straight back to that place. After a while, he was unable to draw me back to that place and I began to feel like...

All this time and energy invested in this one person – my teens and early twenties, my kids – I had been through so much, tolerated so much, I actually didn't want to try anymore. He had me so roped in emotionally to never feeling that things could be anything more than what they had been for so long. I ended up hating him and loving him at the same time! I never thought that could be possible to feel because it should be either one or the other. I wanted to leave him for good because he made me hate him, not only for the things he had done but what he was still doing, but then, because I still had feelings for him, I stayed, so it was a frustrating and complicated cycle.

He would always use the children as his secret weapon to make me feel bad, put on a sad face, hold the children, cry in front of them. "My children miss me." "I can't live without them." Try and make me look bad in front of them, like I was sending him away and all he wanted was to be a family. Then I would catch him looking up to see if I was watching. Their young minds couldn't understand what he was doing.

Writing this book has been great for my emotional development. Once I had completed my story, I no longer felt the need to go ahead with counselling because this book has been a form of counselling for me.

People ask me why I stayed with him.

"Tell me one nice thing he does."

I remember the very first time I was asked this question. My reaction was delayed as I thought about it. The only thing I could think of in regards to having a good memory was spending movie nights with him during the times he was in a good mood. As for why I stayed with him, I had no idea. I thought I loved him, but it wasn't love. It was because I knew no better – had never known better – with my self-worth having been taken away from me completely until there was nothing left but my children.

I didn't want to walk away after I had invested so much of my life in this one person and put so much energy into him. I wish that back then – a long time ago – I had had someone to get through to me to show me that I couldn't have this happily ever after. It's a fantasy that only exists in your mind; not his. People are who they are; you cannot change people. It was never going to be what I wanted it to be, no matter how long I stuck it out.

After Effects of the Abuse

This part of my journey that I'm about to write about is the most difficult, most painful part of my journey.

The children and I were on our way to my friend's home. We had bought pizza and nibbles for her children and mine. My friend's little girl and my daughter are about the same age. On the way to my friend's home, my daughter and my friend's daughter were walking side by side and my friend was walking behind them. As they walked, they began speaking to one another and my daughter said, "My daddy isn't nice to my mummy. That's why he's not around anymore."

My friend's little girl said, "My daddy isn't nice to my mummy either."

My daughter then said, "My daddy's always horrible to my mummy. I saw my daddy strangle my cat. That's why mummy had to send her away. I love my cat, Princess."

My friend called me and told me. I was glad that she had told me so that I was aware she was feeling a lot more than I thought. I had no idea he had done this to the cat, let alone that my daughter had seen him do it. To be so young and to witness what she did must have been traumatic for her.

I sat down with my daughter that night and had a talk with her. I asked her how she was feeling and about what happened. She told me that she misses her cat and that she didn't do anything wrong but, because daddy wasn't nice to the cat, she had to go.

I explained to her that what her dad did was not something people do so that she understood that it's not normal, that it's an awful thing for anyone to do, and that Princess would be happy where she is. I also told her that none of this was her fault and that it's okay to miss Princess.

After Effects for Me

When I came home and closed the door behind me from being out for the day, I would feel on edge. It was normally that initial moment of coming into the house and hearing it so quiet. I would feel paranoid and would instantly check the house. When I say 'check the house', I don't mean entering a room, looking around and leaving; I mean that I would check under the bed, in the wardrobes and cupboards. I would give the house a thorough check before I felt as though I could relax. The emotional scars were there and were now showing me how crazy my life once was, especially how this person had affected my thought process.

Another Day

I woke up and made my son a nice breakfast. He said, "Mum, I have something to tell you." We walked to school together and he started talked about how, not long before I left, his dad, my daughter and I had gone to the hairdressers and that he had stayed with his dad that day.

After I had left, he asked my son if he wanted to play video games with him. He started shouting at him because he blamed my son for erasing all the information that he had saved on the console from the previous game.

He sent my son to bed in the middle of the day. My son went to his room and started playing with his toys. He marched upstairs and beat him with a belt because he wasn't in bed. When I returned that day, he behaved normally.

Guilt/Blame

I hugged my son and told him how much I love him. The first thing I asked him was why he didn't tell me. "You're not in trouble for not telling me but I just wanted to know." He said he was scared of his dad and he couldn't say anything for that reason, but now he knows that he can't hurt us anymore he feels comfortable to tell me.

"I am so sorry."

"This is all my fault."

"If I had made better decisions, you wouldn't have gone through this."

"He can't ever do that to you again as long as I'm alive."

I felt so guilty. I have challenged so much throughout this year, I can handle the things that happened to me and made my peace with it all a long time ago but the idea of him hurting my children was painful beyond words. I wish I had known what he had done back then so that I could have done something about it.

If I had left him and kept him away from the children they would have had better childhoods to remember. It's my job to make sure my children have the best experiences in life; it's my responsibility to protect them.

I felt as though I had failed them. This is all my fault. How could he do that to them? How could anyone be so wicked?

I know my son will always remember that and I cried so much that day, mostly because of the guilt. "Don't cry, mum. I don't want you to blame yourself."

When I left the school that day, my heart was hurting so much. For the first time, I needed someone to give me strength. I prayed and prayed, but I truly felt as though I couldn't rise above this.

"Come on, Mel!"

I picked up the phone and called a family friend, who has had similar past experiences as me. She told me the following, which have given me great strength and comfort:

"You left him with his father, Mel. You didn't leave him with a stranger, so, despite whatever happened, you wouldn't expect him to be ill-treated."

"You didn't do these awful things; he did them, and he will have to live with it."

"You only wanted to make things work."

"It's great the children are so happy. Their behaviour is great, they are doing well at school and they have no difficulty expressing their feelings to you."

"It's good they talk through things with you and, with your help, they will be able to define what's normal for them with your guidance as they grow."

"If your son thought his dad's behaviour was right, he probably wouldn't have mentioned it to you, so it shows a lot for him to talk to you about it."

"It's not your fault, Mel. Stay strong and don't blame yourself. You have done the right thing now for you and them before it's too late for them to have the chance of a normal life."

"You should be proud of yourself; not blaming yourself. You didn't know what he was doing, and you have come through the other side."

Domestic violence is a crime. No woman should have to live in fear of her partner. If you think you may be experiencing domestic violence, you are not alone. Visit refuge.org.uk or www.1in4women.com for support.

"The National Domestic Violence Helpline, run in partnership between Refuge and Women's Aid" – 08082000247